ELIZABETHAN

V

JONATHAN LOVEJOY

The Complete Poems of Elizabeth Peele

Volume V

Armageddon Publishing

Cover: *Young Girl Holding a Basket of Grapes*
Elizabeth Jane Bouguereau (1837-1922)

ISBN-10: 0692319204
ISBN-13: 978-0692319208

For every Elizabeth

Introduction

Carmen Angelina Coletti (Elizabeth Peele) was perhaps the greatest composer who ever lived. After her death, studies of her music revealed a body of work—almost exclusively instrumental—of such beauty and power as to defy description. Even so, her lifelong reclusiveness rendered them obsolete to the world, and these musical treasures may remain apart from public view forever.

Even those few who heard her original scores did so in quiet apprehension, that this beautiful widow—lost somewhere deep in North Carolina farming country—brought forth music as completely ingenious as any ever written before. The sounds of greatness flowing from this woman's piano, surely this is not meant to be! For what purpose can she truly serve as a neoclassical composer in a jaded modern world, except as a curiosity and eventually, a fountain of eternal exploitation?

But while music did serve as a profession for her since she was twelve—her only wage being a sound mind and spirit—there was still another expression, both private and unintentional, equally meant for her eyes only. Gathered posthumously, so few of these "assemblies" can be called unique or special, and likely cannot set her apart from any other lonely poet in the world. But still they live on, as a glimpse into the mind of a musical genius and abused woman of Faith. Written parallel to her music over the years—with no striving for greatness or immortality—these poetic trifles, ironically, may be the only compositions of hers the world will ever hear.

or

"The Assemblies"

Volume V

Such is the grandest music among us—

Poets...

Such are the wildest thoughts among us—

Composers...

The Book of Sharon

601

A sparrow sits on the windowsill
Waiting for winds to blow
A wind of fiery destruction
For every part of Earth

Skies darken in warning
Over a wind that threatens to show
Winds of Eschatology
Voices—

Winds in the key of eschatology
Roaming the earth

Demons at play!
In the world today
With power over the mind

Not delinquents—not truants
Though greater influence
Every human soul in kind

To live is to suffer
To die is gain
Every longing of the heart
Flies to Him again!

A stroll in the green grass
Past the grove of trees
To the mountains beyond the hills
Off to Heaven we go!

604

This woman braved the medical place
Looking for an examination
What she got was a seven hundred dollar embrace
With abject humiliation!

122nd Assembly

"Do you think you're homophobic?"
Said the younger woman to the older woman
The older beauty did not answer
Their world faded out of focus for a second

While she gathered her nerve
At their picnic in the park
At their trip to the carnival
On their walk through the Mall Parking Lot

Their moment alone in the kitchen

Their world went out of focus
For the briefest moment of moments
While the older woman leaned in
To deliver her answer in awkwardness

The younger beauty responded in like clumsy
fashion While onlookers covered their mouths
And opened their eyes twice as wide—
As they were before

606

Wisdom shines the stars of heaven
Across infinity
In beauty beyond reasoning of the mind
For an eternity

The mouse overcame the gerbil
In a bloody war to the death
He seized upon the gerbil's throat
'Til he breathed his final breath

This was our final flame
Our monument to civility
With every mansion and hut the same
Exercises in futility

"Wait for it!" the throng cried
It will be there when you need it
This war will kill every side
If the generals won't concede it!

A science man threatens a call
Hoping to cut my brain
Swaggering shoes in the poverty hall
In from the pouring rain

Medication and restraint
To brighten his dreary day
Avoid the Devil in saint's disguise
More price than what's good to pay!

123rd Assembly

609

Arriving home past the evening day
In the blackness of a Winter's Night
Relatives have arrived to stay
Despite my soul of weary spite

Along the shores of Christmas Eve
They buy decorations for the lawn
Lights and sounds from Horror's Weave
Roaring til the crack of dawn!

610

Horror pains a heart to grief
Images from the cauldron deep
Whispering every dying leaf
A pile of garden mulch to keep

Don't look behind the eyes of joy
There's nothing there to see, he said
I looked with the mischief of a wayward boy
Seeing nothing at all inside his head!

611

Death sits in my room
Disguised as a doll
With his arms crossed—
Waiting

Death is the skeleton of a dead pirate
Sitting in my room
With his arms crossed—
Staring

Its teeth glare in perpetual smile
His eyes blare in perpetual stare
A knowing gaze—
Haunting

Another look reveals a graduation doll
A dog in a commencement hat
A white face where skeleton teeth used to be—
Smiling

Elizabethan V

Death is in my room
Disguised as a doll
Baring its teeth in a dead pirate's grin—
Glaring

Aloft upon The Soaring Waves
Death is gone from my room
Looking for a new soul to
kill— Searching

The shadow of inspiration
Darkens grass of the Great Lawn
Blocking the road to imitation
Others were traveling on

"Is that why you love her," she asked
"For the little words she spun?"
I said "I'm a prisoner of the task"
"Until the day is done"

Abounding promises and whispers
Deep kisses in the chamber
Without the power to dismiss her—
Yet none as well to claim her!

613

Rolling in the drowning rain
Strangers in crescendo
Invading eyes of Devil's Pain—
Trolling by my window!

124th Assembly

614

Faring better than a man—
Some canines have the plan
Never a headache, never a wife
Days unburdened by stress of life!

Claustrophobe slept here—
The walls are closing in But
the poison is kept here
For the day when I say when!

Now Gilbert is the fool
'Cause it happened even once
Unable to abide the rule— In
the panic throes of Dunce!

615

Barefoot-Rank is preference
Than world-wide fortune and fame
If humanity needs your reference—
It will happen just the same!

How do sisters at first giggle—
Then are joined at the hip?
Their sour lives are in a pickle
On this planetary trip

Fruitless days—useless nights
Running to and fro
Dazzled by a Summer's Haze
Entranced by whitened snow

Empowered by preordination
In thy garden—bloom
Hearts are hardened by globalization
Two roses in the know!

617

Sliding a tarp from the grocery place
Regretting my decision
Replacing it in Leisure's Pace
In necessary precision

Helping a tiny tot's misery wrought
Having nack for such a role
The boy said "you did it all for naught"
"Now there's filth upon your soul!"

125th Assembly

The Devil reached up through the floor
And pulled a pencil from my hand
The pencil laughed "I expected more"
"From a man with a so-called plan"

"We've lost it all by now," it said
"No need for a Call of Crying
Everything you do is dead—
So wise up and stop all your trying!"

Golden cisterns on the mantlepiece

Below the break of dawn

Knocking them away to hold the
peace Ashes of the dead and gone!

620

Voices fading in the din
In the colorful room I'm flying in
Being told to hurry—being shown the way
In a photograph crafted on the color wheel

Stocking the warehouse for a rainy day
I saw the lights and colors and sounds revealed

A single spot of crimson
Is blood on a white sheet
A rose in bloom—a frog in a tree
A line through cultured civility

A single spot of crimson
Is the war to end all wars
A river red when it runs
With blood of a billion dead

It is a baby's tears
After the red of its birth Into
a world of snowy white
Expanding to color the centuries

A single spot of crimson
Is sweat from the face in the Garden
It runs from the crown of thorns
To the foot of the Cross

The maple leaf in autumn
The flag in the breeze
Flying over the battlefield
Or a summer field of green

A single spot of crimson
Is the lake of fire and brimstone
The cry of the guilty—beyond the grave
For the shedding of innocent blood

126th Assembly

A spirit hails from Amherst!
To pay my soul a call
She banished every other voice
Beyond the dark'ned hall!

She said to me, "If thine soul be true—
Pay close to whom you hear
Take no gamble with thyself—
Only Divinity's Ear!

Devil tricks and demon play
Make no further heed
If thine light divine's a Pearly Gate—
A fish in water, you'll be!"

Heaven delivered every verse

Whether dusk or dawn

To her grieving room at Amherst

Above her Garden Lawn

She "felt a funeral in *her* brain"

"A fly buzzed when *she* died"

She "measured every grief *she* met…"

"With narrow probing eyes"

"Because *she* could not stop for

Death…" "He kindly stopped for *she*"

From her window at the Homestead

A dying world to see

Her "narrow fellow in the grass"

Be it snake—or sin

Descended as on Muse's Wing

Her mind—her heart—'twas in

Image and voice—word and verse
Into her garden, grew

Like unto the daisy—and the Bee
The butterflies—they flew!

Strolling in her Garden Lawn
Beneath the Flowering Tree

A soul beyond the setting sun—
For all eternity

The morning—the elephant—the lamb—the cat
Hiding in the way
From Adam's garden to Adam's barn
O'er the fields they lay

In storage with the harvest corn
From Green to Gold to Brown
Under the lash—in winter's ashe
In the pain of days to come

Troll the ancient yuletide carol
Clocks me on the run
Success lies at the bottom of the barrel
Until the day is done

625

A tropical breeze from the mountains

An arctic wind from the cove
Skies of fire and ashes
Hotter than a stove!

Take no heed to caution
You won't need her anymore
Civility has been auctioned—
Mankind is no more!

The poetic thread weaves a tapestry
Chosen centuries of doom
Under skies of apocalyptic dread
Woven in Harvest Loom

Slitched in crime without a frozen peep
Cloven hooves running to and fro
Tormenting every soul to weep
In alabaster fields of snow

In the manner of His choosing form
The fabrik of time is woven true
Inside an eschatological storm
Remembering when the sky was blue

Redemption in a pattern sewn
The cloth is fabriked red
When salvation will be bravely shown
In the manner of a severed head

Beyond the number of the beast

When Grace and Righteousness have
flown Kings—paupers—the fairy feast

Mercy corrupted to the bone

127th Assembly

From the past, they drift
People I knew before
Some dead—some living
Casualties of war

No militia—no armistice
No fighting men of lore
Children of a mother—
With disdain for whom she bore!

In the age of logic and reason
With everything on the shelf
Books of toys that come to life
In full animated self

One merely has to weather the storm
While the rest of it goes kaput
Underneath skies of apocalypse
In the rain of ashes and soot!

Oh Christ! Thy blessed relief divine
For this unworthy life of mine
Thy promise to abide!

Send Michael to this earthen
mire To glorify my heart's desire
Oh Savior, crucified!

He resists the proud—but gives grace to the humble
As far as the eye can see
From the grass—the rose—ev'r Bumblebee
To the Crown of the highest tree

128th Assembly

Peaches, plums—kettledrums
Singing from Antiquity
Bloodlines—generations—abominations
Running thru perpetuity

Idols—fools—the Golden Rule
Twirl the flow of time
Eden—enemies—Gethsemane
Troll the evening line!

Teeth gnarled in an angry look
Hair scraggly with regret
Eyes green—glossed over in rage
Trembling with blood lust and craving

Lightning on the nightstand
In the field of fluff and puff
A stuffed bear—with the face of a demon—
Mocking me!

633

A fearful, scary, terrible glimpse
Into the face of Hell
Satan—demons—burning imps
Pain and agony to tell

Strains of Melody Divine! Descend ye angels nine!
Partake thy rhythm and wine, of my Harmony's Valentine!

Oh, Spring was once for lovers, bygone ties of innocence
White rose days hath bloomed and died, under skies of no repentance
Sing the voice of antiquity, Daisy's ingenuity

Consider the Lillies of the Messiah Field, His merciful gratuity!
Meadows of Perpetuity, where Princess Melody hath flown

To lend voice—the billion souls o' mute—beauties never known!
Whirl the wind *Tancredi*, trip the ocean bell to ring

Chords unfurl the Great Music Hall, delight upon thy Muse's Wing!
Vulcan emplodes tutti's pow'r, thundering infinity

Woodwinds swoon the time-line, basses croon the Holy Trinity
Hailed from ivory sanded beach, pizzacato from the briny deep

When the sea bird harps the mountain peak, colors of a Divine promise to keep Whitish alabaster horse, one of fearsome, final four

To strike the Spirit from the Living, onto the apocalyptic shore
Touchstone breathes its final breath, into the empty theatre hall
Now the Great One rises from the depth, to answer unto Destiny's Call
Thumping softly, thy gentle quake, a rumbling beneath the sea
Tears cry pain in deep for Three, Creation—Redemption—Salvation to see!

Fairies skip from branch to leaf, smiling secrets of a tonic soul
Violins laugh, violas play, flutes and clarinets in the preacher's role
Flowers ink the Coletti Pen, lift me up—take me there!
Where Antonio Amadeus hath been, a likeness in silken angel's hair
Behold! He cometh on a cloud! Every eye shall see Him!
When earthquake sings the call to duty, sun and moonshine fading dim

From hills of Olympus to the valley floor, light is dying still
Mysterious harmonies 'voke nature's awe, in iciness of their fervent will
Crescendo's heart awakens to stir, singing to be heard

A message from the Great Beyond, that in the Beginning was the
Word! Lightning in the Music Hall, descended Glory of Christ Divine!

From a tree in the midst of the Garden of Eden, to a Savior's Cross on the
Calvary Line! Now angel's laugh is heard again, violins anew
Echoes of a happy song, in the sorrow of the evening blue!
Clarinet gives her proclamation, aloft in beauty's view
Strings join in exultation, a recompense is due!
Crescendo's heart seeks to stir again, in tiding for a rage
Announcements of the final hour, last of this present earthen age—
Melody resounds the Great Music Hall, throughout the storm of a rising wind
Applauses from here to the Shores of Heaven—at last, mankind has come to end!

129th Assembly

Rains upon the unjust and just
On the poverty wheel
Lust of the eyes and pride of life
Poisoning the deal

Opening the heart
To an unjust rain

Color circles roll the green
Points of life unkindly seen
A future—and the past

Names before the Eden Born
Unrequited love forlorn
Destiny—at last!

637

Ah, to breathe the air they breathe
Blossoms, birds—and every
Bee Spring beckons a soul at the precipice—
Grieving to be free

Sorrow cries in birdsong
In breezes to where I am
Adrift across the wilderness
To the promised land

Magic wand is a pencil
Briefcase is the pillow
Bed is a magic carpet ride—
Tree the weeping willow

Clocks are innocent bystanders
Ticking the flow of time
Avoiding the touch of guilty hands
Of those who do the crime

Unblemished hands of time
Marking every mile
Along the plane of the ecliptic
Prisoners in style

Clocks are casual onlookers
Observing the calender flow
While the creators corrupt themselves
In sin from head to toe

On our blue path among the stars…
Beauty smiles in rhyme A
casual observance— To
Mark the flow of time

640

Peace—serenity—

Where did you go!

In death, perhaps there'll be no pain

Nor suffering to know

130th Assembly

Across the Poverty Field—
The crucifixion was known
Words, sights and sounds
Spread over infinity

Having seen the Messiah
With our own eyes
Having spoken to Him
One month before the shedding of His blood

He seemed to be the handsomest man who ever lived Hidden underneath the whiskers
And the fasting
And the general stresses of His calling

I braved the field of Roman soldiers
On the day they nailed Him to the Cross
On the day his innocent blood was shed
For the sins of the world

Elizabethan V

But even while we wept and
cried For the pain He endured

We know that it was as He had forseen
As He had fortold to us a month before

And I remembered on the trail to Golgotha
The fun I'd had when I looked into His eyes
One month before—
Saying, "You should keep the beard, Messiah"

In His countenance

In the burden of fasting and inner
prayer— There was a smile

642

He put his arm around his friend
"How ya doin'", he said
With his other hand—he took his
gun And shot him in the head

By moonlight—in the mountain
woods He buried him like a winner
He drove back home—he washed his
hands Than sat down and ate his dinner

Thirty years later, on his death
bed The man said, all is well
He closed his eyes and caught the hand
basket Then he died and went to Hell!

A tornado is a woman…

Whirling bold and beautiful

Appearing from a cloud as a puff of smoke

A column of wispy grace…

Turning towards the ground

Visitors to her are left in awe

As she adorns her evening

wear Shoulders bare

Skin of alabaster and silken beauty…

Whirling madness into their brains

The lady begins to rise in Olympian

Beauty Twirling her whim and will

In the skill of otherworldliness

She lays waste to awe

Turning it to a field of rubble
Rising beauty to her cloud of birth
Gently lifting the immovable
Floating it into the air…

Like a feather

644

Love and desperation grieving
At thy station in bereaving
Life and liberty to gain

Poverty shall cease its craving
In sacrifice, a soul to saving
Signs of the Cross remain

Fear of the dreadful public
Shy from beginning to end
Verses shrouded in mystery
Time and time again

Fate gathers words of the recluse
In the manner of a banner flag unfurled
In the storm of appreciation and ridicule On the eve of a dying world

Embraced by the generation of youth
Verses are made to sing
While the word man seeks help for the mind In the Hall of the Mountain King

In fear of the dreadful public
Shy from beginning to end
Beauty smiles golden haired approval
To where the wordman is hiding in

131st Assembly

646

I should like to die in peace
Feeling no pain or sorrow
Only the slightest bit of exhaustion
As though I would like to go to sleep…

And dream

647

There are children on the plane of this ecliptic
Who understand what it means to suffer
Their lives have taken a turn to the macabre
Delivered from the hands of mothers…

And fathers

Parents by blood alone And
not of the spirit or soul

Caring nothing for the ones they bore—
In blood

The lady dances true blue
To melodies from the third heaven
Blasphemies as the morning dew
At the apocalyptic feast to leaven

The lady sings in motherhood
Reminiscing sinful years
Joy and sorrow to the brotherhood
Laughter from the Hall of Tears

The lady dies in beauty
Underneath skies of rain and war
Having done her earthly duty
Escaping what the world is waiting for

In days before Armageddon

People will have fun—riding the
machines Snakes and dragons—wolves
and bears Winding through the woods

Over the rivers and streams
Climbing high into the sky
Plunging to Earth again
Screaming cares into the wind—

And the rain

In days before the skies are reddened
People will ride the machines

In the name of fun and
games Laughing—playing

Delaying the inevitable storm of truth
The realization of who they are
Where they are
And what winds are threatening to blow

But the wind of their ride blows into their faces—
For now—
Taking their breath away
While they ride the machines

650

There is no place I'd rather be
Than my coffin above the ground
While cold attacks a tiger's growl
I rest from the winter whistling sound

132nd Assembly

Fear and disillusionment
Across the prairie plain
Bulls attack in weak resentment
Flipped to the ground in pain

Greatness seeks a new challenge
From the chosen one
Who possesses none of their ability
Desperation frozen on

Fear of the dreadful populace
Appearing on the plain
Beds of sleep and innocence
Up against the prairie window

Wishing for a better time
Working on commission
A charge from above the open plain
In the fires of indecision

There is a certain Murray Perahia

Standing or just sitting there

Calling music from the Great Beyond

Like magic in the poisoned air

From Bach to Chopin to further

on With pleasure on his worthy

key Letting the piano sing its

voice From sea to shining sea

Rise above those trees of life
And tell me what you've got
See that the forest is drowned in fog
Show me what you've got!

The woods are waiting for you
Patience is wearing thin
We await the Second Coming with gladness
And a place for hiding in

Lights go down—the sun comes up
Hidden behind the gray
The fog is visible around the trees
Inthe gloom of the Autumn Day

Peter saw him in the garden
On the eve of the Crucifixion
Running when the soldiers tried to grab him
In the pain of a new affliction

Running across the Garden In
frustration rather than fear
Ready to deny him one times three
As the crows of the morning cock appear

Knowing full well what had to be
What manner and what fashion
Wishing to know it all again
To prevent the Savior's Passion

133rd Assembly

A device would like to be invented

To subtract great size to thin
The reduction of exactly 70 tons
To the size of the head of a pin

Concerns of antigravity
A tube for transporting in
Objects that weigh a million pounds
In a tube like a ballpoint pen

Tons of refuse and rubble
In the tiniest little place
Kept here or harmlessy disposed of
In the coldness of outer space

The Moon will appear as an angel of birth

Carrying children to Earth

Placing them in a Moonbeam

Where they will be safe

Until some lucky passerby finds them
And takes them home
These children are blessed among men…
And women

Having not been born of man and woman
But were delivered upon a Moonbeam
As God's gift to the world

These people are extraordinary indeed
Believing that they are fully human
But they are of angelic origin
Gifted beyond measure

Beyond reasoning of the mind

These are Children of the Moonbeam
Born in joy
Found in peace
Raised in happiness grown

Withhold not thy blessings—

From this unworthy servant!

Lift thine curse from the path before me!

Let Heaven rain its blessing as the Hurricane—
In the glory of thy name!

Television is a window

A portal to a world of stupidity

An endless stream of nonsense

Created for monetary gain

The spewing of artists' pain

To put a stain on the human soul

To make him regret his time on the Earth

It is better to close this window
And look towards the sky
Where the stars beckon knowledge of the
Third Heaven And the coming of the Lord

134th Assembly

Beneath the sphere of lunar white

Is a circle of crimson light
High above in eschatology—
In a sky as black as night

More spectacular than the stars of
Heaven Is the sphere of crimson light
Resting beneath the lunar sphere
In the dark of earthen night

The world views the final sign
On the eve of what they call "The Big One"
When the ground will quake so violently
That cracks will form beyond imagining—

To swallow cities in a jig

Elizabethan V

The sign of the earthquake is coming
In the sphere of crimson light Beneath
the circle of lunar white
In the fall of earthen night

The man of music is humiliated
Stripped down to barest bone
His dignity confiscated
His pride in living stone

In a world where arrogance is king
He walks in humility
Wishing only to be allowed to sing
To children in civility

False accusations are a razor
Cutting the flesh in tow
Cleaning the skeleton like a laser
Bare bones from head to toe

Compassion and a heart of giving
Gifts from Heaven above
A skeleton walks among the living
In naivite and love

From the world stage—*help me!*
The little girl had cried
Rescue me from what I've done—
Help me restore my pride!

I live in the shadows, little one
There's Nothing I can do
How can a Nobody be your lifeline,
There's Nowhere to attach it to!

I saw a little toe tag
Tied without regret
They put me in a body bag
No wine—no Vinegarette!

Assassinated characters
For every eye to see
The Queen of Fungalooga In a
world too harsh for me!

The search for pleasures—ended
Down Cemetary Way
The Reaper is now befriended— In
the cool of the Evening Day

135th Assembly

Sophia will invite words in her cocoon

Does she not remember them?

It comes—and not a moment too soon

The world sings a December hymn!

The Moon—a clown—a crystal blue sky
Cruising the flow of time Friends—
Lovers—a grieving mother
Guilty of a similar crime

In a champagne glass, visions burn
When Earthquake rumbles, Moon will learn
Check it out, darling—it's a million times 3
Wait for lunar rising, sun…

It's as near as it can be!

665

Now that the divorce is final—
Do you remember when?
You laughed and played as a family
Before lust and pride crept in!

The woman is a great composer
Gifted as there's ever been
A talent born from genius—
Heaven—rather than sin

Look to the East—look to the
West No melodies to hear again!
Her piano has grown silent—
Like the coffin she is buried in

136th Assembly

Through the closed door—a spirit comes

Saying, *here now, there you go*

Then the spirit leaves the room again—

Mysteries for me to know!

Cruising the road to Honeyblue
On a motorcycle to nowhere
In fervent concern for what money is due
Grieving for Divinity's love and care

A shadow appears in crimson red
Without comfort but instead
Killing me to the bone—
The most fearful sight I've ever known

Horrors creep outside my room
Such terrors I've never known before
Zero at the bone—
Freezing me into a block of stone

670

Hope is as the setting sun
In mourning to disappear
From worthy and unworthy souls
Grieving to get in

Joy is as the twilight
Fading to evening night
As stars twinkle above the horizon
For a life that might have been

137th Assembly

671

Strolling the library of broken dreams

Looking for a promise—unfulfilled

Best laid plans—hopeless schemes

A soul in grieving left to kill

In the grandest scheme of things
Mercy gives a second look—
Showing where to find melodies
In the tree—or by the brook!

Hidden in the flower garden
Humming—like the Bee
Songs in the highest and lowest key—
Waiting there for me.

I praise the gift of second sight
Divining every wrong or right—
In praises to His Son

While nature blossoms in delight
Bees and hummingbirds take flight—
To honor the Chosen One!

674

Violence and depravity is racism—in security

Prejudice in the land of peace

Passive hatred in the guise of purity—

Tasting *prosperity* in their soul's release!

138th Assembly

675

The Nubian Warrior is commissioned
On the eve of a nuclear age—
Implanted with knowledge of Tomorrow's Yesterday—
Printed on the ambiguity page!

676

A family of crows invades the palace
 Dressed in leather and linen
Looking for death in the eyes of the King—
While condescension tickles them to grinning!

Beauty that can cause pain
Agony—severity
Eyes, the nose—the lips again
'Fusing with impurity

Aversion to a reflection
In the mirror lives
The heart of suffering is her beauty
Insecurity—it gives

Where does Joy live?
I would like to go there
If only for a visit
With neither worry—nor care

In my prayers, I pray that she
Would come to visit me
I'll look for her at the window—
Will she be there today?

139th Assembly

I felt a raindrop—

Though I've not seen the sky in many a year

Was it the weeping of an angel?

The blessing of a tear—unseen?

Loss is gain—
Through grieving years
Its good to hear laughter—
In a world of tears

Ghosts stop by
From days of lore
Repressing memories—
Of times before

681

Though kisses be sweet
They can be ineffectual;
Leaving the bearer without—mercy
Absent of dignity

Choose one, they said—for a battery of tests

One soul is what they are after

Through begging—the volunteer is left unchosen

Completing—his—furlong—to—

Disaster

140th Assembly

Jupiter is thy name
Ruler of the Gods
Burning like the dimmest star
Turning with envy

Desiring warmth of life
And the Beauty of souls
Clouds o'er a barren, lifeless terrain
Concealing thy domain

The Grand Waltz flies brilliante—
Above perpetuity
A white dragon with azure eyes
Breathing a blue flame

A dragon as white as a cloud—
Eyes as blue as the sky;
A dragon named Sylphides+
Breathing blue fire

Her flight is something to see;
From the Black Mountain across the ocean,
To where they live and breathe

The wind whistles her musical flight
Rising in a voice of song Descending
the power of beauty
To cover the world in flame

Forests burn colors of the Ocean
As she dances on the wind
Her wings to carry her aloft
And take her home again

Truly as wayward children

Who cannot cease from sin

Like the bull in the china glass shop

Perilous times—therein

The man is locked away from the world

With no need for survival

Told by the angel—*don't die*

From this apocalyptic Earth

The man searches for relief—

Finding only ridicule

While the future remains untold—

Unknown

141st Assembly

687

Athletes jumping to and fro
On the uncertain field
Sending possibilities high into the air
To sow the planter's yield

Clocks and blackbirds—ticking away

To mark the flow of time

Families' heart—no days to start—
Never to undo the crime

Shirts spread out—tinted green

Linen shrunk to December

Images from a little girl lost

Too disturbing to remember

Doors click—angels drift away

Mercy for those in need

Care for the sick—and indigent

A blessing for their greed

They decided for the radio show
To see if they passed the test
If their marriage could survive
ridicule And derision by the best

The media man made fun of them
In the manner of a genius clown
'Til their laughter welled up with tears
With pain and sorrow pouring down

Messages in Carolina Blue Then
the blue of the Aegean Sea
Printed in lack of
communication— Indisputably

Teeth smile in false politeness
To the couple from Agora
In the age of knowledge and reason
On the eve of the Aurora

The media Man bade farewell
To the S.A.D. man and his
wife A thirty minute record—
Of unrequited life

142nd Assembly

691

Stolen for a few days
So he could see where it's at
The horror of being as ordinary—
As a common alley cat!

I spoke to the man of mountainous music
To inquire of this gift
Knowing whenceforth the harmonies came
And melodies adrift

There are chords that flow as rivers
Somewhere outside of time Waiting
to be irrigated
By a spirit thief sublime

Music flows as a river
Toward the eternal sea
Stolen from the land of dreams—
To this reality

Hellfire looms like a hearth—
Burning our names into its chest
Appearing in the midst of church service
Paradise for the living

A place hot enough to melt lead
And boil iron in seconds
Flames of extraordinary account—
Waiting

Flames that can be heard if you listen
Burning like a hearth
Embers of rock instead of wood—
Glowing

Rising as a cliff of glowing stone—
Orange with fervent heat
Burning hottest underneath churches—
Waiting

Elizabethan V

Souls screaming to
God Creating lies—
Repeating lies—
Causing pain and heartache to their own

Crucifying the innocent—
In modern times
Believing the worst about the Music Man—
Unguilty

Whose brothers had fathered children of
lust Exploding bombs of strife about
To devastate the reputation of the Music Man as
well Who had fathered none of his own

Running through the trees of autumn
Down roads of Endtime's Way
Strolling into the mouth of the city
Into the traffic of the Latter Day

Hell burns like a hearth
Glowing orange and fervent heat
Waiting for souls in the God-life
To awaken

Words—a Mountain—a born Desire

To be gifted as to say

Voices confined—volcano fire
In the Earth to stay

A prisoner of want—sorest need

To "Golgotha," in a word

O'er land, the sea—to the Forest Breed

'Til every—eye—hath heard!

People, a problem! T'will ever be

As certain as the sun

The Moon, the Star—the Honeybee
Weep for the Chosen One!

What fun—here—to lie at rest
Beneath the waiting soil

A pillow, a cushion—a new suit—the best!
A living death to foil

143rd Assembly

In the early evening breeze
Spring touched by summer's calling
Blossoms rain from trees of rebirth
Falling to the ground

White blossoms running, tumbling—
Rolling over the ground
Given life by the warm wind
In the early evening breeze

Trees in mourning for beauty lost
In joy for that they gain
Promises of a summer leaf canopy
Growing in the spring

Drawn to Earth by its beauty

Visitors arrive

Carried through the atmosphere—on a whim
On free will

Riding through the air—

Dressed in black

On vehicles that float

Gliding to the ground

The beings are standing up

With arms out in front

Holding handlebars—

Floating through this space

This time

They render attack null and void
Without effort

While they speak a message of peaceful coexistence
And the end of our age

Appearing at the Vatican
Along with the whirlwind
To anounce their intentions—
Of peaceful rule

Understanding that peace is not
possible In a hostile takeover

The soul of violence is black
Seeking to destroy what it needs
What it craves
What it desires

What it longs for is blood—
Pain—
And tears

699

A roar—

A woman's face splitting in two

A scream for the ages—

In burning

144th Assembly

700

Golden yellow skin—
Caramel eyes
Bosom to infinity
A fool's disguise

701

Pain has a red head—lit by a flame
Or by striking into fire
'Til the red begins to burn

In this hour of burning
The flame gives off amber
Illuminating a heart's agony
A soul's despair

Words given through birth of fate
But having no affect
Bringing pain to the daughter of misery
A mountain of regret

Aesthetic lust brings disarray
To the house in Poverty's Field
Coins thrown in Frustration's Way
Rolling across the floor

Coins roll the light brigade
From the sofa to the wall
Fallen from hands of disillusionment
With no further tolerance at all

Evening falls over stability In
the manner of a setting sun
Above the house where frustration rules
And victory is never won

The residents have fought the fight
To get to the other side
Growing weary of pain and strife
The husband and his bride

145th Assembly

704

Some of us shall not sleep
Some of us will be changed
With no time in the coffin
above Or in the ground below

The Prince lies in testate
With a smile upon his face
With a twitch and a stifled yawn
For all the world to see

The prince has not been embalmed
Due to a royal request
Now consequences threaten resurrection—

From foul play

The prince was buried alive, they say
In a moment of fidelity
Buried asleep inside the coffin—

Where he will awaken

He used to say, *I despise thee*
In the spirit of fun and jest
Now he lies in fidelity—

With a new burden on his chest

Scary to the maximum
While having a bit of fun
Skin as sweet as caramel
A tasty sugar bun

Sporty to the maximum
No maliciousness or harm
Beauty unburdened by vanity
Athletic grace and charm

Ginger to the maximum
In hair aflame of fire
Voluptuous in *girl power*
Burning with desire

Baby to the maximum
Innocence in tow
Locks of glimmering, shimmering
gold Candy kisses sweet to know

Elizabethan V

Posh to the maximum
Glamorous and pure
Skin of alabast 'n ivory cream
Lovely and demure

A wave approaches like a mountain
Devastating the forest trees
Frozen with nowhere in the world to run—
With weariness in the knees

Hearing the trees snap like
sticks In the power of the wave
Trying to comprehend my burial—

In a watery grave

146th Assembly

Yellow swans—blue swans
Red swans—pink?
Speculate what colors the feathers were
Of those that have gone extinct!

Peking man—peking duck
What is it that we know?
Feathers of Archaeopteryx
What colors did they show!

What pattern was the T-Rex—
From his head down to his toe!

709

Very beautiful, emperor James

Now go home—

And give me my family

But I thank you just the same

710

A disassembly of pieces

The puzzle—my life

711

She stands in the twilight field

Gazing at the setting sun

An angel as a winged dove
Alights to call her home to glory
On reverie—a Spirit's flight

When the story of her life is done
Standing in the twilight field
Gazing at the setting sun—
To remember days of bygone life…

147th Assembly

712

At the top of the flight of stairs
Does it still go around and around?
The answer—uncertainty
Now the halls seem smaller

Not as difficult to navigate
As they did before

713

Children play,

Until they are murdered

714

Images of a former life
Painted on a mountain
Shining bright in the light of day
While longing springs forth a fountain

At the edge of the suburban woods
Ghosts from a former life appear
Strolling toward the house of the living
Compassion for souls in residing here

715

Jailbait—out of bounds
Misery to avoid
Stalemate—a bout of rounds
The forbidden to enjoy!

148th Assembly

716

I don't know—why ask me?
There's nothing I can say
I don't know why your life is cursed—
In such an epic way

Step through the walls—stroll the field
Lie down in the open grass
Gaze toward the third heaven
Let the accursed hours pass!

717

Like fire from a lightning sky
Emotions burn inside
In the mouth of a crazy, lazy cat
A tiger's roar opened wide

They need to find a place to live
Hopefully—and soon
Somewhere to finally call their own
Beneath the Harvest Moon

At the edge of the open farmer's field
Hoping for a life
Weary of the city lights—
A young man and his wife

They need to find a place to live
Beyond the Winter's Cave
Tiding the wave of Poverty—
To escape an early grave

719

Thunderheads—from the sky to Earth
Threatening a fall
Prophecies gather in a gray sky
Rumbling a storm

Whispers of fulfillment
In the forest trees
Implications rising—
Like a flood

149th Assembly

720

The music man outside my window
Waiting to get in
Longing for his innocence
To take him home again

721

The number 503
Looms over inadequacy
On the eve of choices made

Nighttime forests—
Houses—stars
All hope begins to fade

Claustrophobe—clocks
Dark'ned windows—
Living in the shade

Bedroom prisons
Coffins—graves
Recompences paid

Strawberry preserves—
Peach preserves—
No orange marmalade!

A melody of unearthly ingenuity
Wrought by angelic skill
Born to a fool with no memory
Lost on Amnesia's Hill

A concertino for Piano and Orchestra
Like none ever wrought before
Displayed as petals of the Rose
Rossini through the Modern Door

The Orchestra of Carmen Coletti
Joined by her piano key
Genius from the gates of
Heaven Lost for eternity

723

It was the dog in him that did it,
Causing him to look around
Sniffing from pillar to post,
His nose along the ground—

With a whiffing from pillar to post
With his cheating nose upon the ground—
To another's arms, he was surely bound

He was merely a desert, he giggled
Full of dead men's bones
You pledged your heart to another
So you should probably leave me alone—

I think it would be best
If you were to leave her and me alone

Your wife is home, waiting alone

150th Assembly

724

Dost thou labour in vain

To build a monument to nothing?
Shall I cease this hopeless plea
Looking to destroy me?

Outside the window—down the road
In a dark'ned night
A foggy road leads to nowhere—
Shall I travel on?

725

Such is the grandest music among us
Poets
Such are the wildest thoughts among us—
Composers

Blessed with the gift of Muse

726

A giant figure—rising high
To scare me to Perdition
Doing nothing in assistance
To my nervous condition

727

Two souls lost—beneath the seven sisters

Looking beyond their life

Wishing to know where they must go
To avoid turmoil and strife

Rising high above every nation

A tree is known by its fruit

The seed of the Redwood is mountainous growth

While the Sequoia looks down upon them

Trees to make the world bow with envy
Bowing to another

A Tree known by this fruit of Growth
Reaching toward the Heavens

Towering above the Redwood

Rising like a mountain

All roads lead to Sequoia

To where Creation is ruled

Jonathan Lovejoy

All roads lead to Sherman
Towering above the Redwood
Creation rules infinity—
In the Forest Grove

Eyes of the werewolf—do beckon at the door!
Threatening to come in
The lycanthrope waits under a moonlit night
To devour those in lust and sin

The sound of the werewolf—at the door!
Growling to get in
To make quick work of every innocent
soul Time and time again

In a shack--in the Mansion—unprotected!
When the moonlight of death shines in
The eyes of the werewolf are at the door—
Burning in the Fire of Sin

151st Assembly

729

Snatching away—an overly mountain'd paradise

Granny is from the Hills

She'll break your neck and thank you twice
For giving her a soul to Kill

Whipped until your skin is bleeding

In the manner of her own *amour*

Acid covered lightning sticks—

To burn your skin some more!

730

A circle in the third dimension
Is a perfect sphere
Built to collapse in upon itself
Then to re-form again

Colors of Beauty on one side
Shades of white, red and green
Colors of the Triune Godhead
In perfect Beauty and Power

On the inner side of the sphere
Is a surface of melancholy gray
To represent the artists' pain
And the futility of his way

But the sphere collapses in upon itself
To reverse the rainy color scheme
To display the colors of hope to the world—
In glory—redeemed

Being driven through the land of the dead—
Past the forest grove of trees
Seeing the newly planted growth in waiting
Threatening a promise

On this road to nowhere
Through the Great Tree Forest
An angel in ambiguity
Burns a gaze into my eyes

This—
Causing me to wonder
Whenceforeth comes this being?
Angelic or demonic?

Assuring me with a stare—
Of my own uncertainty
Reminding me intrepidly—

Of my own inadequacy

Elizabethan V

Speeding the road to nowhere
Through the forest grove of trees
We pass the simple and the dispossessed
On their walk toward freedom—

Coming from no special place

A prisoner of what is meant to be
Wanders among those unaware
Looking for a doorway
To the land of the living

732

She cooked herself a life meal
A fresh and tasty treat
Lettuce—tomato and cheeses
A treat so good to eat

She made herself a life meal
And ate it 'til it was done
Hamburger, seasoned perfection
On a fresh and tasty bun

Each part was health and glory
Carbs—protein galore
She marveled the taste of every
bite Until there *was* no more

She cooked herself a death
meal And ate it all alone
They found her brains on the refrigerator
Splattered with blood and bone

733

This is insane, the doctor's girlfriend said
As she kissed her lover on the lips
Sweetly, the doctor returned this—discreetly
While squeezing the flesh of *her* lover's hips!

152nd Assembly

734

Tom Cruise—in the world of Minority Report
Regretting his decision
With talent—disguising epic disinterest
In Spielberg's futuristic vision

Searching his mind for clues and signs
Of this future living on his own
Wondering why the whirlwind took Nicole away
Leaving him empty and alone

Love has no gender
No race or religion

Falling from the Throne of Grace
To touch every heart and soul

Of this—every spirit is able
As children of the Most High

In the way of He who gave his
life— For the sins of the world

Rossini is still my number one
The father of modern music
Melodies of manic ingenuity
Born from a heart of amusement

Muse was his welcomed companion
More often than not t'was she
Operas crafted with a bolt of lightning
For the entire world to see

Rhythm and Melody from another realm
Bouncing in through my window
From 1810 'til the present day
His orchestra burns fiery Crescendo!

The Golden Iris is the key
To unlocking the womb—
Where secrets of the universe are held
To decorate my grave 'n tomb

Questions abound—why?
What truth cuts like a knife?
That a man should leave his mother and
father— And cleave unto his wife!

Symphonies 1 thru 5 appear
Burning ingenuity
Unable to see their uncertain future—
Churning incongruity

Symphony No. 1 is Power
Ordered from Divinity
With a name above every other
name Blazing through infinity

Symphony No. 2 is Meekness
Forged in fire of pain
Crafted harmonies from a Family
Tree Drowned beneath an autumn rain

Symphony No. 3 is Beauty
Whispers from a heart of prose
Music played on Depravity's String
In painted colors of the Rose

Elizabethan V

Symphony No. 4 is Truth
Flaming azurean white
As the end time falls from a Prairie Sky
In the chill of a summer's night

Symphony No. 5 is Death
In blue and black fire of Hell
With hands of innocence stained in blood
Abominations and Wickedness to tell

739

A mountain girl sings a melody
Yellow Roses from her mind
Beauty touched by her desire
To leave poverty behind

A family curse of generations
Is broken by a song
Love and joy—to a million souls
Her melodies belong

153rd Assembly

740

In Satan's memory book

He wrote down what I had done

When I winked at the exotic sales lady

And said "*Just rememberin', Hon*"

Then, the Accuser took it before the
Lord And showed him when I had fun

The Lord said, *"He's covered under the blood..."*
"For everything he's ever done!"

741

A long, lonely trip to tomorrow
Looms in the walls around me
Waiting to choke my spirit with poison
Then hang me with rope from *Ennui!*

742

The dance of the fairies
Skipping the garden trail
Carried aloft on winds of beauty
Above the flower veil

The voice of the angel—
Along the valley floor
Rising the heights of their longing
Among the heavens to adore

743

She would like to kick up her heels

The Plain Jane hussy of a wife

Desiring to be with other men

To vex her husband's soul to strife

The Angel appears in lavender
Cloaked in silhouette
To send verses to my Dying Day
In the Hall of Modern Regret

Mothers and daughters engaged in battle
In a cage upon the Great Lawn
While seeds of doubt are laced anew
Down the Road of Disillusionment we were traveling on

Rest while the ceaseless billiards play
In the auditorium of the walking dead
Listen to the voice from Amherst
Sing the sixpence song of talking dread!

I cannot praise the spider
Nor hail her fearfulness grown
Where others might discern of nature's beauty
I find they are best left alone

Elizabethan V

I see the bride and her bride's maid

Lost down Beauty's Way
In the loveliness of perpetual agony
On the eve of my Dying Day

745

Angels move you along the way
Aiding your decision
Giving comfort and guidance when they are needed
To formulate thine artistic vision

In the Palace of the Gold Leaf
Transferred to the next level of being
Greeted by an infinity of the blessed ones
In the place where believing is seeing

Looking toward the Great Horizon
Where beauty calls a heart to grief
In days where uncertainty seeks to crumble
Inside the Hall of the Golden Leaf

4th Assembly

Driving a golden car at night
She swerved to miss a cat
A cat with glowing, yellow eyes—
Now Death is where its at!

The cat trotted off into the night
She breathed her final breath
She lived to see it vanish from sight
Then closed her eyes in Death

Any fool who traveled this road at night
Was cursed with a similar fate
As a cat walked out of nowhere in the dark
With glowing yellow eyes of Hate!

747

A military drill
Sounding off among the hills

The morning jog—no time to kill
The recruited *figure*—a bitter pill!

Bouncing—bounding
Mounds of it in pounding
Jealously abounding
When the recruited *figure* comes around!

She jumps—she crawls
She runs—she falls
Doing her duty—that's all!
No mercy from her fellow soldiers—

With hardly a speck of it at all!

Old Man Pervis was his name
A farmer, to be sure

A nice man who praised hard labour
day And the style of its allure

Exhaustion crept into my soul
On the Eve of his determined labour

I slept when I should have been at work
In a manner entirely unlike a neighbor

The old man smiled and said, *no problem*
Don't worry about it, son

So I relaxed from the pain of fruitless
toil Until sleep and exhaustion were one

He had to agree—I didn't have a pied
piper Then he said, *you've got to get pied*

I asked him—what manner of nonsense is this!
And he directed attention toward my left side—

Elizabethan V

He showed me a weaving spider's web
Attached from the room to my pride
He smiled while I ripped the giant web away
In a fright so severe I could have died!

But the lonely trees have been in waiting
For this terror to have begun
For me to die in the web of the spider
And leave a mountain of hard labor undone!

Drums ensnare the soul!
Nature comes where thunders roll…

Dance thy bolted lightning shears, for tears the Clouds of Heaven
Rivers grown through years bereaved, living bread for souls to leaven
Fair rhythms laugh thy strings bemuse, infused by Jove's frivolity
Amusement threatens their earthen gate, laid bare thine untold equality
Prance a two-four melody—pitched high into the sky—
Above the clouds, to the edge of night, bewitched developments decry!
Keys lowered to the valley floor, waiting to arise again,
Return of Laughter's cloak disguise, where Bassoon in Echoes fading in

Drums ensnare the soul!
Nature comes where thunders roll!

Rain pours upon Wicked's Horde, to swell each and every Earthen Sea
Doors sealed by Divinity's Hand, Volcano spews of thine decree!
Oceans rise where peaks divide, waters climb where mountains be
Fountains rumble the mighty deep, whirlwinds above their ship to see
Woodwinds in league with Mockery, disdain for vile Debauchery
Hopping a disarming Harmony—voices warning what ought to be!

Elizabethan V

Tides lift in Crescendo's Way, terror falls to bended knee Lightning
crashes skies of fury, thunders blast the Judgment Key! Daisies,
tulips, roses bloom, in the garden of the Honey Bee
Happiness seeks a bereaving room, to Homestead beyond Antiquity!

Cry, my sweet, thy tears, Ninetta! *The Thieving Magpie* takes the ring! Golden
harmonies from Heaven's Throne, melodies for a grieving bird to sing!
Valleys rise, high mountains fall, weeping Hall of the Shepherd King Swing to
a rhythm in the flow of time, obey thine call upon the lightning string
Give homage to his fleeting calm, live Glory to this blessed thing
Bow thyself the voice of wrath, tremble before what Seven Thunders bring!
Clarinet, Bassoon, Flute and Horn—whispers of thy doom to moan
Atonality's breath in Violin's repose, to arise from slumber and creeping bone
Now pendulum swings Heaven's home afar, falling down to Water Stone
Swinging low, past the sea below—thru painted colors in nature's tone
Lifting up the sounds of beauty, streaking light in powers grown
Delight in slipping sparks to fly, by the petal blossoms of flowers known
Lightning strikes in blue and white, whirl the lights of Glory shown
Birds in chorus for what they know, whistling harmonies to the Judgment Throne!

Now iniquity rolls the bloodline, Creation through the heart of Eve—
Laying blame at the serpent's feet, the demon root doth sin alleve
The blood of Christ, do thine soul to ease! Look to Heaven for this sole reprieve!
At the foot of the Cross, let Redemption be, Salvation to those who must believe!
Back and forth the waters sway, lost upon the ocean deep
Braved beyond their day's relief, in the burden of bereaving hearts to weep
Play the song, Love's Humility! Pray for the peace of eternal sleep
A Sinfonia in the clouds above, Melodies of His Divine Promise to keep!

750

Strains of genius fill the air
In the land of no appreciation
Overtures two centuries come and
gone Displayed before a modern nation

Attitudes of intolerance
Roaring through Agora's Lair
Surrounded by those who wish them harm
Too filled with Lucipher to care

751

Elizabeth? Can we leave this place?

Yes, Love. We can.

Where can we go?

Far away. To a place we've never been—

To a place we can call home.

752

Living in a foreign land
Looking for a space to own
Insults in an unknown tongue
Throwing filth like I have never known

Returning to the Halls of Poverty
Grieving for a place to roam
Claustrophobe emerges from the walls
To create desire for a better home

ABOUT THE AUTHOR

Jonathan Lovejoy is a graduate of the University of North Carolina at Greensboro with a B.A. in Religious Studies, and a graduate of Liberty University with an M.A. in Theological Studies. He currently lives in Winston Salem, North Carolina.

For more info on the author's life and career, visit jonathanlovejoy.com.

www.ingramcontent.com/pod-product-compliance
Lightning Source LLC
Chambersburg PA
CBHW060919040426
42445CB00011B/690

* 9 7 8 0 6 9 2 3 1 9 2 0 8 *